Ring Ready

Ring Ready

A Practical Playbook on How to Find, Keep and Marry Mr. Right

---

Jena Janse

Mahanaim House, LLC

JenaJanse.com

LIBRARY OF CONGRESS CATALOGING-IN-PUBLICATION DATA has been applied for.

Jena Janse
Ring Ready: A Practical Playbook on how to Find, Keep and Marry Mr. Right
Edited by: Charlina Allen Pruitt
Published by: Mahanaim House, LLC

ISBN: 0-692-16898-2
ISBN: 978-0-692-16898-1

Printed in the United States of America

While the author has made every effort to provide accurate Internet addresses and other contact information at the time of publication, neither the publisher nor the author assumes any responsibility for errors or changes that occur after publication. Further, the publisher does not have any control over and does not assume any responsibility for third-party websites and their content. This book is not intended as a substitute for psychological or medical advice. The methods described within this book are the author's personal thoughts. Any use of this information is at your own risk.

DEDICATION

This book is dedicated to three amazing women:

To: my mother Jenesta Messam for awakening the wife in me by being a constant example of Proverbs 31.

To: my mentor Stacy Cox for challenging me to either be an entrepreneur, or work for one.

To: my friend Malaika Williams for helping me realize my gift and encouraging me to operate in it.

I thank you. I honor you. I hope to make you all proud.

CONTENTS

FOREWORD
By: Enitan O. Bereola II

START HERE

There are no bad decisions in dating - there are only lessons. Bad decisions lead to better choices. Tests become testimonies. Mistakes mature into morals. Heartbreaks lead to headaches. And after the aspirin is your lesson.

Congratulations, you're a healthy human being.

Kiss enough frogs and you'll get your prince because breakups guide a bride to her intended groom. But the lessons in this literature aren't solely about leading a lady down an aisle. Oh, no - if you purchased this book for that and that alone, please return to sender. Whether you're in the bedroom or boardroom, your standards should guide you to never compromise on your bottom line. This literature is a lifesaver that prepares you to be the best version of yourself for yourself, your peers, your partner and your purpose. Period.

So sip some wine and read between the lines. Avoid viewing this odyssey as only applicable to romantic relationships. Whether you choose to be single or married, the journey to becoming a wife prepares you for the journey to becoming the best you. Being dope isn't exclusive to dating. And having a date doesn't make you dope. Character makes you a catch. Don't grow weary in well doing or be discouraged by the current climate. If you lose yourself along the way, it's OK. Your journey to self-discovery will always lead to love if you keep going. Let your flaws inspire you to try again each morning. The inevitability of consistency is growth. No matter how small, each step in the right direction is progress. When you begin to trust in your decisions, you affirm yourself. When you affirm yourself, you gain a greater level of confidence in your abilities. When your mind is in agreement with your soul, and your soul agrees with your body, you have taken the steps to fall in love with yourself.

I can't convince you to be patient, kind, forgiving, humble, honorable, generous, fair and protective toward your mind, body and soul. The journey is personal. Life offers up opportunities to act in love daily. I can only make you more aware in these moments. The decision to respond requires discipline and understanding. Anyone can love you - but if you don't have the capacity to love yourself, it taints your ability to properly love someone else.

But don't worry about all of that. We've considered you while writing. I've thought about you while focusing on this foreword and the author constructed an entirely beautiful piece of literature from a lifetime of work - for you.

Go ahead and pour a final glass of wine and prepare your heart, mind and soul to be changed forever. If you're destined to marry, don't dare close this book before saying, "I do." If you're undecided, you've already opened up to this page, so open yourself up to the possibilities of love and all that it can do for you, him and the world. Love is that powerful. Love doesn't love for a reason because love is void of conditions. Love is.

The only condition is this: don't plan your wedding before you plan your marriage; otherwise, go ahead and plan for your divorce.

INTRODUCTION

To the woman reading this book, you are amazing, you are beautiful, and you are more than enough. Embrace who you are today at whatever stage in life you are because you are still evolving and the woman you are today will be unrecognizable to the woman God is refining you to be. Enjoy the waves of change. Learn to appreciate your failures and celebrate your wins in a major way. Don't compromise on who you are, your values or your integrity. Never settle for less than you ask for and never give more than you can afford to lose. I hope this book encourages you to demand the respect you deserve, not only in relationships but also in life. Landing that diamond ring and waltzing down the aisle is not the pinnacle of success. Your worth is not defined by your marital status but by the status of your internal joy, and your happiness starts with you. Your peace starts with you. Your relentlessness starts here.

The purpose of this book is to wake up the wife in you. It was written to help you realize the magnitude of who you are in Christ so that you act according to your purpose, not your past. This book will teach you how to get everything you want without compromising everything that

11

you are. You will learn principles that will make you more successful in relationships and give you insight on how to avoid the common habits that delay relationships from progressing to the engagement stage. The book is broken down into three parts. The first part of the book will explore how to attract the right man. The second part of the book will focus on how to keep a man's interest after the attraction has been established. The third part of the book will demonstrate how to get a man to commit to you, without having to ask him to. I would recommend for women to read this book before they start dating and to re-read the book once they are in a relationship so that they can get the most out of the concepts. Everything taught in this book is supported by real-life examples of how I implemented them in my own relationship, which led to my husband proposing to me almost a year after we started dating.

While I was writing this book, a certain event in pop culture happened: one of the most eligible bachelors in Hollywood, Idris Elba, proposed to his recent girlfriend just a few months after he had said in an interview that he never wanted to get married again. Every blog was buzzing with the story and people took to social media to ask questions about the "secret sauce" this woman must have had that caused him to change his mind. While the media was focused on her beauty, wardrobe and accolades, no one mentioned her character. The whole ordeal was entirely frustrating because I'm sure if we got the chance to ask her what her "secret sauce" was, she would simply say, "my standards." I fear that women in today's society are being indoctrinated with false ideas of what it takes to get a man to commit. With an increase of fake reality shows and false Instagram influencers that seem to have it all, a lot of weight is placed on image, sexuality and social status as a means to securing the bag, the king and the ring - but it's a lie, which is why I decided to reveal my story. I had to learn the love game the hard way and made many mistakes en route; however, there are a few truths that I did learn: your lipstick won't get you noticed, your laugh will. Your perfect waist won't get you a second date, making him wait will. Your body won't make him fall in love, your boundaries will. Sex won't get him to propose, standards will.

I want to share something with you. I, too, was subconsciously being programmed to think that I wasn't enough, and that I had to give something up for my relationship to level up. My previous relationship had left me broken and unsure of my worth. Believing I had no value, I allowed men to treat me the way I thought of myself. I eventually realized that what was happening in my life was a result of what was happening in my mind. So I made a conscious effort to get out of my mind and into God's word. I sought scriptures that affirmed my identity in Christ and I spoke them over my life daily. What I found in God was healing and restoration. I was reminded that we are gems. We are precious diamonds and sometimes we allow ourselves to fall into the hands of people that can't see us. My love, your value doesn't decrease based on someone's inability to see your worth. You can't expect a man without vision to cherish a diamond; for all he knows, it's just a rock he'll eventually toss back into the wilderness. But the beautiful truth about rejection is it's actually God's protection. Listen to this - sometimes God will allow you to be discarded to keep you hidden in the rough until He sends the right person to discover your sparkle and polish you off.

Every moment in this book is a result of my journey from broken to whole, and single to married. While the lessons I learned along the way did allow me to assert myself in relationships, God is the not-so-secret sauce that made this formula successful. I don't get the credit for any of this. I didn't discover anything new. I didn't reinvent the wheel. I simply added God to the equation and everything started to add up. You do the math.

This book is the evidence of how I used the insight that God gave me and applied it to my relationship. God is the reason I was complete before meeting my husband, and because of that, I was ready to be found. God is the one who directed me to make the move to a different country, which ultimately led to my husband finding me. God is the one who used the people that He did to orchestrate the events that led to me meeting my husband. God is the real MVP and reason behind every amazing thing that has transpired in my life and I can't wait to see what He is about to do in your life.

I hope you enjoy reading my story. As you read it, don't be anxious about getting to the next phase of your life. Enjoy your journey. When it comes to inheriting the promises God has for you, there is no race and no competition. What has your name on it has already been set apart.

Regardless of what your journey entails, no one can take what's been promised to you. You are someone's blessing. You are someone's good thing. And someone, somewhere, can't wait to make you his wife. Whether you know it or not, you are the answer to someone's prayer. May you always recognize the favor that you are.

Love,
Your Sis in Christ

PART I: HOW TO FIND HIM

CHAPTER 1
WHAT IS YOUR "WHY?"

"Why" is always a relevant question to ask. The answer reveals reason and exposes purpose. The ability to uncover your "why" in every area of your life will lead you to the most significant discoveries. This chapter aims to help you discover your "why" in the area of love and relationships. Look for the correlation between your reasons and your results and you will understand the importance of aligning what you want with why you want it. You might have picked up this book because you want to get married but what I want to know from you is why you want to get married. Your answer will determine "what" you do and "where" you go, which will influence "who" you meet and ultimately affect "when" you get married.

The type of people we date are often a direct reflection of our reasons for dating - or lack thereof. Have you ever thought to yourself, "Why on Earth did I ever date that person?" We all have. The simple answer is you shouldn't have been dating in the first place. Below you'll notice three familiar fallacies to break down some of the wrong reasons people jump into relationships along with advice on how to avoid these traps:

Social Media Simone – is a beautiful, ambitious girl who feels like she is missing out on life without a relationship to flaunt on social media. What Simone doesn't realize is in this age of social media influencers where people's relationships can be used as a platform to be monetized, some of the relationships that she sees online aren't real. Some of the relationships she admires have ended long ago but they are still posting pictures and hashtagging #couplegoals just to get likes and gain followers. If you are like Simone, and the reason you're seeking a relationship is so that you can post cute couple pictures on social media, then you aren't looking for a partner, you're looking for a platform. My advice to you is to limit your time on social media to pursue your purpose. Don't jump into a relationship because you want to compete with people you don't know. Get to know who you are; date yourself extensively. How can you physically date yourself? Simple - start by writing yourself love letters. Buy yourself gifts to celebrate personal victories and have the gifts professionally gift-wrapped. Schedule dates with yourself that don't include Netflix. Your solo dates can include taking yourself out for dinner, going to a movie, a museum, anything; just set a date and show up on time, wearing and looking your best. Pursue you; do something every day that will cause you to fall more in love with you.

Nympho Nikki – is well-educated, moving up in her career with a great social circle, but wants a man to fulfill her strong sexual desires. It's common for people to end up in relationships that stem solely from a desire to be pleased sexually but doing so isn't wise. Sexual stimulation causes neurotransmitters such as dopamine and oxytocin to flood the central nervous system and alter our neurochemistry. Oxytocin is the chemical commonly referred to as the "cuddle hormone." After sex, the release of oxytocin causes its subjects to want to cuddle or sleep with one another, creating a feeling of connection or attachment. Dopamine is one of the chemicals responsible for the high people get on certain drugs. Ever hear the saying "Sex is like a drug?" Well that's probably why. Dopamine is released during sex and it activates the reward region in our brain causing a euphoric feeling of achievement, which tells the brain you have done something good and should continue to do it. After sex, it's easy to think you have a strong attachment to the person but the feeling is just the hormones reacting to stimulation. After sexual relationships have been formed, they can be difficult to end due to these hormones that have tricked your brain into believing you are feeling something deeper than you actually are. What you might think is a strong affection for the other person can just be an addiction to a feeling. There is a reason God designed sex to come after marriage; it's a complex process and its effects last longer than the act. If you're in the same position as Nikki, my advice to you is to get yourself a B.O.B. (battery operated boyfriend). The Saints would have my head for that one. But on a serious note, don't date someone just because you're sexually frustrated; trust the process and wait for Mr. Right. I know better than anyone that waiting is hard - no pun intended. It's especially difficult if you have already been exposed to sex. Desires are strong and the flesh is weak, but God is a sustainer and greater is He that is in you, than he that is in the world. Slowly wean yourself off sex by committing to sexual abstinence. Start slow; commit to two months of abstinence. If you are successful, reward yourself with a gift and then commit to four months of abstinence. As you make it to each set time frame successfully, reward yourself and recommit. Let a trusted friend know about your decision so that they can keep you accountable.

Lonely Lisa – has it all but just can't seem to find the right one. She is tired of being the third wheel when she goes out with her friends and their partners. Lisa sometimes finds herself entertaining guys that she knows aren't good for her because she is lonely. If you're feeling like Lisa, my advice to you is to get yourself some new friends. No, you don't have to dump the old ones, but find some new people to hang out with that won't make you feel like you're missing out on something. Don't give yourself the opportunity to be bored. Boredom breeds recklessness. Take up a new hobby, travel and go to self-development conferences where you can meet and connect with like-minded women.

People get into relationships for the wrong reasons all the time. In fact, most people don't even stop to think about what the right reasons for dating are. Dating is defined as "a stage of romantic relationships in humans whereby two people meet socially with the aim of each assessing the other's suitability as a prospective partner in an intimate relationship or marriage" ("Dating," September 7th, 2018). So the reality is, if you aren't dating with the intention to build a life with someone, why exactly are you dating? For most of us, the first person we date doesn't end up being the person we marry (and that's OK) but we should still date with that intent. And while the purpose of dating is to be a catalyst to marriage, the purpose of marriage is to propel procreation. And although procreation is scholastically defined as reproduction - typically referring to the production of offspring; I define procreation as: "the product of when two people come together in faithfulness to give everything they have indefinitely to create something good that can be given back to God for His glory." The reason I redefined procreation is because I know many married couples that can't have children; however, through their marriage they have created incredible ministries that are changing lives and ultimately giving God glory. This is what marriage is all about. It shouldn't just change you; it should transform everything and everyone around you. When you look at a prospective partner, you shouldn't see what they could do for you in a relationship; you should look at them and see everything you can accomplish together that will ultimately give God the glory.

In the past I've definitely dated for all the wrong reasons. I was Lisa, Simone and Nikki at different stages in my life. After I had gotten my heart broken, I started dating a guy that I knew was bad for me. He had no good intentions and he made it clear that he didn't want to pursue anything serious with me but I didn't care. I felt like because I got cheated on that God somehow had cheated me, so I went on a sin spree. Of all the wrong reasons to date, trying to get back at God for something He didn't do is probably the worst reason, right? I was trying to heal a hurting heart but all I was doing was cheating myself out of real healing. It didn't take me long to realize who I was and what I wanted. When I discovered that, I stopped entertaining people that weren't in alignment. I didn't want to be a side chick, baby momma, or someone's lover - I wanted to be someone's wife, so I dated with discernment. When someone asked me why I wanted to be married, I could say without hesitation, "I want companionship that is a reflection of God. I want to come together with one person and give them everything I am, to create something good for the glory of God."

Before you start dating again or entertain anyone in the idea of a relationship, make sure that you have determined your "why." Allow yourself some time to really understand why you want to be in a relationship. Your reasons don't have to be like mine, but if the reason you're dating doesn't line up with the purpose of dating, and subsequently the purpose of marriage, then don't date. Take time to figure out what you want out of your love life. If you are in a place where your "why" is clear and aligned, then be intentional about who you allow to take you on dates. If his reasons for wanting to date don't line up with yours, then don't pursue anything with him. A man's "why" will determine his purpose in your life.

CHAPTER 2
THE LIST

Just about everyone who knows me knows that I always talk about "the list". I'm the type of girl that is easily distracted, so I have to intentionally make myself focus on tasks at hand, and one of the things that keeps me focused are lists. I make lists for everything. I have a grocery list, a to-do list for my home, a to-do list for work, a list of short-term goals, a list of long-term goals, and the list goes on - pun intended. Obviously, I can't be the only one that relies on lists because there is a built-in app dedicated to writing lists on every smartphone. Ironically, all the years I've been making lists, it never occurred to me that I should make a list of the things I wanted in a relationship, or husband. When the realization dawned upon me, it was as if a light bulb went off in my soul that changed my perspective on dating, and ultimately changed my life. If your question is: can you manifest your way into love? My answer is yes and this chapter will demonstrate how writing down your heart's desires can magnetize your itches into existence.

That corny Santa Claus slogan is real: making a list and checking it twice is how to find out if your next man will be naughty or nice. Saying you're looking for a good man but not knowing the qualities of a good man is counterproductive.

Figure out the qualities you are looking for in a husband and write them down. If you are serious about wanting to get married, then get serious about the type of man you are trying to attract. As the law of attraction goes, what you focus on is what manifests into your life.

Not having a list can cause you to end up with someone that isn't in alignment with what you want because without a blueprint it's easy to be distracted by attraction when you should be looking at characteristics. I didn't realize that one of the reasons I kept ending up with the wrong guy is because I had never even identified the qualities I wanted in the right guy. I was just dating based on emotions and we all know that emotional decisions are rarely ever the wisest ones. Understanding this is a lifeline in relationships because as women we tend to unknowingly compromise our standards. If you don't have clearly defined standards to start with, what do you have to uphold? Having an idea of what you want in a husband represents your standards and knowing what you want eliminates the temptation to settle for what you don't want. Have you ever gone to the grocery store with the intention of only buying four items, so you don't bother to write them down? But when you get to the store, you end up browsing through all the aisles just to see what's new and leave with a cart full of things you don't need and didn't come for. This happens on repeat. If you had just written the four items down, it would have provided you a specific purpose, which would have subconsciously directed your choices. You would have gone straight to the aisles you needed to be on and left without diversion. The same philosophy applies to dating. When you have a specific list of the things you're looking for in your ideal man, you tend to not detour in the direction of people that don't match up.

When I speak to single women, I often ask if they have "their list." After explaining what "the list" is, several of them respond, "Yeah, I kinda have a list." But when I ask where they keep their list, they say, "It's in my head." If you are one of those ladies, I beg you to stop! I'm sorry but you don't have a list in your head. You have thoughts in your head and thoughts that can be swayed quicker than a silk press transitions into an Afro when touched by water. Your list will not be effective unless it is written down. It has to be tangible. It must be something you can see and go back to as a reference point. Preparing a list prepares you for a purpose. Your list represents what you are putting into the atmosphere and what you put into the atmosphere is exactly what you'll end up getting.

When I finally understood this simple philosophy, I immediately went to the notes app in my phone and I started writing out my list. The note was entitled "What I Want In A Husband." I wrote non-negotiables down, then I erased some preferences, then I added priorities. The process took a while because I knew I had to be specific. Eventually my list was complete and I felt empowered because now it wasn't just a matter of knowing what I didn't want in a husband; I finally knew what I did want. The beautiful thing about knowing what you want is you don't settle for what comes close. When I was single, I would glance over my list every few months just to remind myself not to settle. When I look back at my list now that I'm married, I laugh to myself because as specific as my list was, it's exactly what I ended up getting in a husband. And while I promised I would never show anyone my list, I'll make an exception for you and allow a peek.

What I Want In a Husband:

Tall
Good looking
Well-dressed
Well-spoken
God-fearing
Loving
Nice teeth
European
Attentive
Spoils me
Faithful
Loves to travel
Ambitious
No children
Drama free

Now don't get me wrong, I'm not saying that my list made perfect sense, or that your list should look anything like mine. Yours should be specific to your desires but this was MY list. These were the things I was looking for in my husband. And it tickles me now when I look back at that list because the man God sent me is the very depiction of what I wrote down: a tall, loving, handsome, well-dressed Dutchman that loves to travel, treats me like a Queen and loves God.

Interesting how that happens, huh? I sometimes wonder if I had not been specific with what I was looking for in the first place, would I be married to the man I am with today? So don't feel self-conscious about anything you write down on your list because it's your list intended for your eyes only. Don't show it off or compare it to another list. Don't get your girlfriends' opinions on what it should contain. Don't seek approval on what you're seeking in a partner. Be true to yourself on this - your list is to keep you focused and in alignment with the direction you see yourself going in. Putting your wants and needs into the atmosphere magnetizes what you speak to flow into your life.

Once your list is done, identify the negotiables and non-negotiables. Negotiables are traits that you can live without, things that are not critical to your happiness in a relationship. Non-negotiables are absolute deal breakers. Just to give you an idea, a few characteristics on my list that were negotiables were superficial qualities like being well-dressed or tall. These were things I was attracted to but not having them wouldn't have been deal breakers for me if my Mr. Right didn't meet that criteria. My non-negotiables, however, were attributes that I wasn't willing to compromise on, like God, fidelity and ambition. Identifying your negotiables and non-negotiables allows you to stay focused on your standards without dismissing potential people that don't match the superficial qualities on your list. You wouldn't want to pass up on a great guy with brown eyes just because your list includes "blue eyes." The purpose of a list is to keep you focused, not restrained. Your guy might not check every box, but as long as he matches up to the qualities you aren't willing to negotiate, you will be in good shape.

If you are currently in a relationship and have decided to make your list, don't make it based on the person you are currently dating. Instead, make an honest list of what you are looking for in a husband. If the person you are currently in a relationship with doesn't line up with your list, especially the non-negotiables, then you have some decisions to make. If you are single and have taken my advice and created your list, congratulations, you are headed in the right direction and I'm confident that you are well on your way to attracting the husband you desire. In the meantime, don't be afraid to meet new people. Go on dates but keep your list nearby in a smartphone so a nice smile and tight abs don't distract you. Your standards start with you; no one else can define them for you and no one else can maintain them for you.

Write out your list on the following page:
Be free.
Be you.

CHAPTER 3
BLOCK AND DELETE

I'm sure you can guess by the title where I'm headed next, right? After a chapter dedicated to recognizing what you want in a husband, it should come as no surprise that the next step is to get rid of any relationships you are in that don't match up to the qualities you want in your future partner. If you are emotionally involved with someone that you know there isn't a future with, chances are you're in a situationship that will only delay you from heading in the direction you need to be going. The key to finding Mr. Right is first getting rid of Mr. Wrong. This chapter reveals how toxic relationships can hinder your personal growth and block opportunities for relationships of value to exist.

I don't need to define what a situationship is in this day and age, but for the sake of clarity, here goes: Urban Dictionary describes a situationship as "a relationship that has no label on it, like a friendship, but more than a friendship, but not quite a relationship" (Derosa, April 5th, 2014). I personally love the way Aidan Neal described it in her blog, "Happy Is The New Rich," where she says, "A situationship is basically a pseudo-relationship - a placebo masking itself as a formative relationship. It smells like a relationship, it sorta looks like a relationship, and it may even feel like one, but it's not" (Neal, August 6th, 2014). When you hear it broken down that way, it makes you think, "Well, that's plain stupid. Why would anyone want a dummy version of a relationship?" But the reality is, if you're adulting in the 21st century, you're either in a situationship right now, have been involved in one before, or you know someone who is stuck in one now.

These pseudo-relationships are emotionally dangerous because one person is typically more invested than the other (generally women), which gives us false hope that if we stick with it, it could blossom into something more. What's wild is women tend to be loyal to the men they are in these pseudo-relationships with, passing up on potentially great guys in the process. If you're in a situationship, or any relationship that you know won't progress into a happy, healthy relationship, my advice to you would be to end it. If you did the work from the previous chapter and created a list, then you already have the blueprint, so let go of anyone that doesn't match up. End it and don't leave any doors open; don't keep in contact; don't say you can remain friends. Keeping in contact with exes, booty calls and situationships are just as dangerous as remaining in a relationship with them. It confuses your spirit and stunts your emotional growth because in the back of your mind there is still the possibility that if you just remain in his life and be a good friend to him someday he will wake up and realize that you are in fact the one for him. Newsflash, sis, you're not the one, the two or the three for him.

Rid yourself of toxic waste and exercise your right to block and delete him and anyone else that is holding you hostage emotionally. There is no reason for you to remain in contact with them. You don't need to follow what they are doing on social media and you shouldn't allow them viewing access into your life either. I know you want them to see you out here living your best life, but giving them access to your page gives them access to you, and that can cause more harm than good because when they see you happy and doing well, they will slide right in your inbox feeding you lyrics and disrupting your peace. Block and delete anyone that is stunting your emotional growth. Your glow up is for you, not for him. You don't need to keep him as a Facebook friend or as a follower. Someone that hurt you should not have direct access to you and your emotional space 24/7. Be intentional about protecting your peace and be in control of who you allow to have access to you.

Allowing the people or person that hurt you to be constantly connected to you will only hold you back when you are trying to move forward and attract the right people in your life. In an age where communication is instant, a simple text message can alter your emotions causing a shift in your attitude and mood. Let me give you an example. Let's say you're headed to work and you receive a direct message from your ex that reads, "Morning beautiful. . .love the new pic. I hope your day is as amazing as your smile." You read the message and smile; and then you start wondering, "Maybe he really is changing; he never meant to break my heart anyway. Maybe I shouldn't be so hard on him." Meanwhile, the really nice guy you met at the coffee shop sends you a text message three hours later that says, "Hey, how's it going?" You roll your eyes and dismiss the text. What you don't realize is the good guy's text only annoys you because it was sent after the emotionally disruptive message you received from your ex this morning and now you've subconsciously compared both men. You reread the "Hey, how's it going" message and think, "Well why wasn't he thinking about me first thing in the morning? See this relationship would never work anyway; he doesn't even give me compliments. I mean would it kill him to tell me that I'm beautiful?" As you roll your eyes and dismiss the text message from the good guy, a pattern starts to form. Without you even knowing it, your ex has just cock blocked you from seeing potential in a great guy because you are focused on a superficial idea of what you think communication is by unknowingly comparing the two messages. Allowing yourself to be emotionally available to people that don't deserve that privilege can distract you from seeing potential in the people that do because you subconsciously compare new to old. Comparison isn't only the thief of joy; it's a barrier to progression. I'm speaking from experience with this. When my husband and I had just met and we were in the communication stages, I tried to talk myself out of being with him so many times. I would go to our mutual friend and say, "This isn't going to work; he doesn't text me often enough, he doesn't gas me up and tell me the kind of things I'm used to hearing; he's just, ughhh I don't know." So this friend asked me to describe some of the things I was used to hearing from guys. When I did, he said, "So you want him to be like the loser that cheated on you?" It was only after he said that, that I realized how ridiculous I sounded. I wanted to pass up on substance because I had gotten so used to empty lyrics. When I realized this, I unfollowed my ex on Instagram, blocked a couple of people on Whatsapp, and unfriended some people on Facebook. I protected my emotional space from the clutter and confusion and it allowed me to see clearly, to date without distraction. Today I am married to my best friend, the same guy I was willing to pass up because he didn't have enough "swag." What I had to learn is that he did have swag; it's just that his swag was different and to appreciate it I had to stop comparing him to everyone else.

At some point you are going to have to take stock of the people who are in your life and eliminate the ones whose time has expired. It's like cleaning up. You open your fridge and toss the expired items that can no longer add to your health. But would you bring a bag of garbage back into your house after you've already taken it out to be collected? Absolutely not, that would be crazy and it would stink up your humble abode. Think of your emotional space as your home; don't bring things back into it that have already been removed for a reason. If you are serious about finding love, you have to part ways with the people who are holding you back from it. Cut ties with them, block and delete them on every medium you use to communicate with them. This is a tough thing to do but it's important that you take the step to declutter your mind and heart. Sometimes that means your phone won't ring for a while and that's OK. Get comfortable with the silence; it won't last forever.

CHAPTER 4
WOULD YOU DATE YOU?

Now that you know what kind of partner you're looking for and you've cut ties with the time wasters that don't match your blueprint, you, my dear, are ready to put in some work. Are you ready to get your hands dirty? This chapter is where the rubber meets the road. This is the game changer. Why? Because this is where everything begins. It all starts with you. This chapter is about self-assessment and self-development. It's about becoming the superhero you are seeking - becoming Misses Right before looking for Mr. Right because you have to become the best version of yourself before you go looking for the best in someone else. If you are lacking anything internally, you will be looking for something in someone to fill that deficit. The truth of the matter is no one can do that. This is the most important step in the book because once you are right internally, everything externally falls into place. With that being said, I hope that this chapter motivates you to become what you are looking for and to focus on being whole and complete before you do anything else.

So my first question for you is, are you holding yourself to the same standards as those of your dream guy? Would you date you? No, seriously, based on the list that you created at the end of Chapter 2, how do you match up to your wish list? This question matters because of two simple principles: the first is that if you embody the qualities that you're looking for you'll be able to recognize it when it appears in your life; and the second is, when you possess the qualities that you are looking for, when it finds you, it will complement what you already have as opposed to completing you. Falling in love with yourself first is the most important step in the quest to getting someone to fall in love with you; love begets love, so if you truly want people to fall in love with you, love must already reside within you.

Now, let's talk about your list hypothetically. Let's say you're looking for someone who is well-educated. That's great, but are you well-educated? What have you done within the last three years to develop yourself intellectually? I understand that everyone isn't in a position financially to pay for higher education but you don't have to hold a degree to be well-educated. There are many ways to educate yourself and expand your knowledge. Read books; attend seminars and workshops for a change up in scenery. Subscribe to business newsletters so that you are up-to-date with what's going on culturally and economically. If you're attracted to educated men, educate yourself with the resources that are available to you. If you're looking for someone who is physically fit, but you're currently overweight with no plans to live a healthier lifestyle, there is a problem. Yes, I know that you are fearfully and wonderfully made, but that doesn't mean that you shouldn't hit the gym and eat more healthily. Now let's be clear, I'm not saying that you can't attract a lean, muscle man if you're on the fluffier side because the man that God has for you will find you and love you at whatever size you are. What I'm challenging you to do is to make sure that you are in a place where you love your physique so that you aren't looking for someone with those qualities just so that they can inspire you to do the same.

When I created my list, I realized a few things about myself. I wanted a man who was drama-free but I was actually very controlling, which was a turnoff even to myself, so I had to work on letting go of the idea that things always had to go my way. Another one of the qualities on my list was that I was looking for someone who would spoil me. So while I waited for my husband to find me, I decided to spoil myself. I took myself on solo dates, which I learned to love. At first it took me a while before I could go to a restaurant and say, "Jena, party of one," but when I got used to it, I loved the confidence it gave me. I ordered everything off the menu that I wanted and I really took the time to treat myself. This is something I challenge every woman to do. If you are uncomfortable in your own company, how can you expect other people to be comfortable around you? In addition to me wining and dining myself, I bought myself beautiful flowers, and candles, and everything I enjoyed a man doing for me I did for myself. I enjoy luxury goods, so I decided once a year I would treat myself to something nice if I achieve all of my personal and financial goals for that year. The first year I did that, I purchased a Louis Vuitton tote bag, personalized with my initials on it. I love that bag and I wear it all the time, even now that my initials have changed. Part of the reason I love it is because it reminds me that I don't have to rely on someone else to be spoiled. And when I did eventually get into a relationship, I didn't settle for less than what I was already giving myself.

Other qualities on my list were "well-traveled," and by the age of 25, I had already traveled to over 15 countries throughout the Caribbean,

Central America, North America, Europe and Asia. The point I'm trying to make is that by the time my husband found me, I had already become the kind of person that I was looking for, so not only was it easy for me to recognize those qualities in him when I met him but most importantly, I didn't rely on what he brought to the table to complete me because I was already complete on my own. Yes, you read that correctly, my husband didn't complete me because I lacked nothing. I was already whole but he did complement everything that I already was. He is the perfect yin to my yang; he is my partner and my best friend. He makes me very happy, very often, especially when he puts his dirty laundry inside of the hamper instead of right next to it. I love being around him. Doing regular, mundane things with him become fun just because of the dynamic we have but he isn't the source of my happiness. I lived in a state of happiness before we met. Had we never met, my life would probably look much different right now - and now that he's arrived, I can't imagine doing life without him. However, had he and I never crossed paths; had I still been patiently waiting; had I still been single - I would still be happy. Your partner should complement you, not complete you. It's the idea that someone can mean the world to you without being your entire world. Leave room for yourself.

I pose one final question: Are you whole and complete? People tend to use these two words interchangeably but they are quite different. Oxford Dictionary defines the word whole as "in an unbroken or undamaged state; in one piece" ("Whole," n.d.). Whereas, the definition of complete in Merriam-Webster Dictionary is "having all the necessary or appropriate parts" ("Complete," n.d.). I use these words in tandem because you need both to really experience a life of joy. A life of joy requires us to be unbroken, with all the necessary parts, so it's impossible to be complete without being whole, and to be whole is the opposite of being broken, which means that wholeness evolves from healing.

If you are reading this book, chances are you have been through relationships or situations that have hurt you in some way, and ultimately left you broken. I have been there and it's painful because it's hard to see beyond your brokenness. The only way to become whole again is through a process of healing. In Japan there is a unique form of pottery called Kintsukuroi, which is the art of repairing broken pottery with gold or silver lacquer, understanding that the piece is more beautiful for having already been broken. What I love about Kintsukuroi is that instead of discarding the broken pottery, the artisans reinforce each broken piece with gold so that the final product is not only stronger than it was before it was broken but also more beautiful. When I think of this, I think of God's amazing healing power. Sometimes we feel worthless when we experience rejection, hurt or brokenness but we have direct access to the only Potter who is able to put us back together. The One who created us. And just like Kintsukuroi, once we are healed, we become more beautiful and much stronger after we become whole again. So don't hide behind your brokenness; find your healing. People often use the phrase "time heals all wounds," and while time does allow for certain moments in history to be forgotten, time can't mend, heal or make you whole. You have to be intentional about your healing. Be as intentional about your emotional healing as you would be if you were physically ill. When I was going through a season of brokenness, seeking God in fervent prayer is what brought me to emotional healing. As I drew closer to God, He drew closer to me. If you find yourself in a similar state and you aren't sure how to pray while hurting, here is how I prayed my way to wholeness:

"Lord, mend me where I am broken, heal me where I am hurt, remove any bitterness and hate, and allow only love to reside within me. Restore my peace and my joy; help me to be whole and complete, loving who I am because I am created by You, in Your likeness. Develop me into the woman that you have called me to be, I am ready for your transformation."

My challenge for you is to examine yourself. Are you whole and complete? Would you date you? If you answer *no* to these questions, then stop right here and focus on wholeness. It's not time for you to find Mr. Right just yet. Focus on your healing. Step into your wholeness. If your answer was *yes* to my questions, then you will enjoy the next chapter where I teach you how to find Mr. Right - better yet, how to get him to find you!

CHAPTER 5
WHERE DO YOU WAIT?

In today's society most people have given up on finding love "organically" because instead of making conversation with the stranger next to them in a public place, they would rather pull out their smartphones to show love through likes and comments to strangers on social media. The fact that social media has played a role in the demise of our social lives has definitely impacted the way people form relationships today. This chapter isn't about bashing social media because it is in fact a remarkable tool when used properly, but I do hope that this chapter forces you to see above your screen. Nonetheless, in a world where communication is mostly digital, and the saying "we met through a mutual friend" usually refers to an online dating service, the questions still remain: how do I find a man if I'm not into online dating and where do I find him? Hang in there, sis - this chapter will give you the insight you're seeking.

"Girrrl, how did you find him?" was the number one question my lady friends would ask me following the news of my engagement being that most of them knew I had only been dating him for a short time. When people asked me this, I always got a little uncomfortable because I felt like they were waiting for me to give them some highly secret algorithm that would blow their minds. The truth is, it was very simple. The secret to finding a man is to stop looking for him. And as underwhelming as that sounds, it made all the difference in my life. When I met my husband, a relationship was the last thing on my mind. I mean, I had my list and was in a good space emotionally and spiritually, but I just wasn't looking for love. As a matter of fact, I had just gotten out of a situationship, so meeting someone was the last thing on my mind. It was during that time when I had finally stopped searching that God decided to send my husband out searching for me.

Just think about losing your keys for a second. The feeling is frustrating, isn't it? You desperately look everywhere ripping through your purse with no luck, and then empty your bag. Your vitamins, lipstick, hairbrush, tampons and 40 other items are now on the counter, and still no keys. After frantically tearing through your entire house, you decide to just stop looking and take a rest on the sofa. The minute you sit down, you see them in the corner of your eyes. Immediately you want to curse the stupid keys but the feeling of gratitude quickly overtakes the feeling of frustration because you no longer have to search. That's how love is, the minute you stop looking for it, it appears out of nowhere; and while you want to scream, "What the heck took you so long?" you will feel blessed and grateful that it finally found you in God's perfect timing. See, incredible things find us when we aren't searching for them.

God doesn't need your help with matchmaking; you don't have to help him look. He has done more with less, so it's time to just be still. This might be the last thing that you want to hear but you have already put in the work. You know your "why," your intentions are right, you have declared the things you want through your list, you have cut ties with the people who were disrupting your peace, you are whole and complete, and your happiness is abounding. Now it's time to wait and watch the manifestation. God knows who will be best equipped to handle your heart because He has already handpicked him for you. There is no need to help Him look because your husband isn't lost; he is somewhere going through a necessary process of preparation for you. All you need to do now is wait but what you can do while you wait is make changes to where you wait. What I mean by that is, sitting at home watching the clock and listening to Joel Osteen isn't going to get you married. I'm sorry, but your hubby won't find you in your house. What are you doing while you are waiting for God to show up with your husband? But more importantly, where are you waiting?

Where you spend your time directly impacts the type of people you meet. I know people seem to believe that the best place to find a good man is at church, and this may be the case for some, but there are also a lot of great God-fearing men that may not attend your church or they may not be a part of any church at all for whatever reason. Newsflash, sis, God can deliver your husband to you outside of the church. Please understand that I'm not discouraging you from going to church. Going to church is a good thing; that's where we are fed spiritually, and we are called to gather together with other believers to worship, to hear God's word and to serve. But your sole purpose for going to church shouldn't be to find a partner, and the only reason I say this is because I don't condone the idea of anyone using the church to pursue a personal agenda. Don't serve in every ministry in hopes that you will catch the eye of one of the deacons; God won't honor that. Let whatever you do be done with a pure heart and good intentions. Likewise, just because you're waiting in faith doesn't mean that you can't have a life outside of church. You're not any less loved by God for having a social life that extends beyond your small group or your church friends. It's OK for you to go to activities outside of church. It's OK to go to social events at bars. It's OK to hang out with people that don't share your faith. The places you go don't necessarily have weight on your walk with God; your heart defines that.

God took me to a different country and placed me in a new job to position me to be found by my husband. Three months into my new job, a coworker, who is Muslim, invited me to a get-together he and his wife were having at their home. I obliged. I arrived at the party and noticed that everyone there was a couple (either married or engaged) except for me and the other perfect stranger in the room who is now my husband. When I think back to that day, I can't help but smile because it was a total set-up and I didn't realize it then, but God used a Muslim couple to bring two Christian people together, to fulfill a plan; that blows my mind. It just goes to show that regardless of race, religion, nationality, we are all God's children and He doesn't discriminate. It's important to never overlook anyone because you lack the capacity to see how he or she fits into the bigger picture.

God's plan for your future is better than anything you could come up with on your own because His ways are higher than our ways and His thoughts are higher than our thoughts. God can use anything and anyone in any place to accomplish a purpose and fulfill a promise.

So you want to find a man? Great, then stop looking and start doing. Stop hanging out with the same people all the time and stop going to the same places. Break your routines. Step outside of your comfort zone, explore new places, do things that you've always wanted to do. Just because you're waiting on God's promises to come to fruition, doesn't mean that you should be waiting in isolation. Where you wait is just as important as what you are waiting for, so book the trip, take the class, go to that party. Why? Because to get something you've never had, you have to do something you've never done.

PART II: HOW TO KEEP HIM INTERESTED

CHAPTER 6
DARE TO BE RARE

If you have been following my advice thus far, then I'm sure you're well on your way to meeting bae. As you step outside of your comfort zone and begin to meet new people and go on dates, I want you to remember that you're the prize here. Regardless of who he is, what he has, or how he looks on paper, he needs to win you over, not the other way around. This chapter serves as a reminder for you to be your authentic self from the beginning of a relationship because being you is the best thing that you could give to anyone else. The Bible teaches us that a man that finds a wife finds a good thing and obtains favor from God. There is a wife inside of you and a man will be blessed just for evoking her. Do you realize the magnitude of what you are? You are the favor factor, sis; you are someone's blessing - someone's good thing. That makes you kind of a big deal, so take that pride with you on every date without losing sight of who you are and whose you are.

The first few dates are important because these dates determine whether there will be future dates or an opportunity to pursue the relationship further. During this time, it's normal for women to want to put their best foot forward, but this chapter is about winning your man's heart by doing nothing other than being your authentic self. You aren't campaigning to be elected wife. He, on the other hand, needs your vote to make sure he is elected husband. Don't water yourself down during the dating phase. This is no time to play Mrs. Perfect; this is the time to be real, show your flaws, show your weaknesses, and most importantly, reveal what makes you rare. I know it's easier said than done because the desire to be liked by others is natural. Although civilization teaches us to hide our flaws and to conform to societal tendencies in order to be liked, this chapter is proof that being true to you is the only way to succeed in relationships. And while you being yourself may cost you some relationships, it will never cost you the relationships you're meant to have. So don't change who you are to gain anyone's approval; the right person will find perfection in your imperfection.

In a society where likes on social media give people more gratification than anything of real value, it's more important now than ever that we become OK with not being liked. You aren't going to be for everyone because your best qualities are hidden from the sight of those who can't appreciate your value. The fact that God will reward a man just because he has found you shows you how special you are. Now is the time to be unapologetic. And yes it's fine to look your best on dates to impress the person that's taking you out, as long as you don't start auditioning. Don't try to be what you think he wants or needs; just be you; your authentic, rare self. You will win every time when the only person you're acting like is you. You hold the cards here and the man God has for you will see the favor factor within you.

One of the first things people tend to do nowadays early on in the dating phase is social media stalk their new boo to gather insight on them. I know we're all going to sit here and pretend like we don't do that, but if this doesn't sound familiar to you, let me give you an actual scenario. Tiffany met Mark the other day and they really hit it off. They exchanged phone numbers and are arranging a date, but Tiff wants to make a good impression and thinks, "Let me look at his Instagram page real quick to see where he hangs out, what kind of food he likes to eat, what kind of books he is reading, etc." Tiff's little social media phishing expedition went from looking at a "few photos" to looking at pictures from 32 weeks prior, hoping and praying she doesn't accidentally hit the like button and give herself away. Social media stalking a potential partner can be dangerous because you can easily fall into a pattern of wanting to identify a person's interests so that you can portray your interests to look similar to theirs to establish a deeper connection. In Tiffany's case, she has now stalked an hour's worth of content from Mark's page and has figured out that he has recently gone vegan. Naturally, the next thing she does is post a cute photo of herself eating a salad with the hashtag #cleaneating. The big issue here is that Tiff knows good and well that she hates vegan food!

You might laugh at Tiffany's scenario but I used to be just like Tiffany in many cases. See, I thought I had to be like someone to be liked by someone. It didn't dawn on me that I had developed this terrible habit in relationships until I was around 25 years old. After several toxic relationships, I realized that I was the main contributor of the toxicity within the connection because I always changed who I was to suit the relationship I was in at the time. When I was dating a Puerto Rican guy, I started dressing differently, changed my favorite genre of music to reggaeton and my interests were all of a sudden the same as his interests. This trend continued as I bounced from relationship to relationship. I mean, I literally had a personality to match every partner. Crazy right? I guess I didn't realize that being my authentic self was enough. It took a while but I eventually learned that you would never have to change your core or alter your personal preferences to be loved by the right man.

When I realized that I was doing myself a disservice by minimizing who I was to make men comfortable around me, I decided to fix my crown. I decided that I couldn't afford to minimize who I am - not for men, friends or even for job opportunities. So instead of being a mediocre version of someone else, I was just going to be the best me. After all, no one else can pull off the gig quite like me. I discovered I am funny, smart, kind and genuine. I mean, who wouldn't love me? So by the time I met my husband, there was no changing who I was. When we went on dates, I laughed loudly when we were in public places; I passed on the foie gras and oysters (yuck) and opted for a burger, or whatever I felt like eating. I spoke my mind and shared my truths. I was unapologetically, authentically, me whether he liked it or not because I knew that there were only two outcomes, either he would love me or he would leave me, and I was happy with either. I was so content with the woman I had become and confident in who I was in Christ that it never even crossed my mind to try to like what he liked or be what I thought he wanted me to be. Much later on in our courtship, I asked him why he fell in love with me. He said because I was different from anyone he had ever met and that he loved that I wasn't a "yes woman", that I didn't agree to everything he thought. I had my own opinions, challenged him at times, and stood for what I believed in always. Isn't it funny how the things that cause some people to dislike you are exactly what makes others love you? For the sake of transparency, I'm not going to sit here and pretend like I didn't cyber stalk my husband when we were dating because I did. The difference is I wasn't keeping social media tabs on him so that my interests could line up with his or so that I would be able to like what he liked when we had conversations. I followed him on social media to make sure that the person he was portraying himself to be online was consistent with who he was offline. I wanted to be sure that what he was sharing with the world lined up with what he was sharing with me in real life. I was protecting my heart.

I have to admit, writing this chapter was uncomfortable for me because I thought you might judge me. I figured you might think that because I used to be like Tiffany I must have been shallow or had some sort of a complex growing up. In fact, I had a great upbringing with parents that did a phenomenal job raising me in a great home with lots of love. My parents instilled a lot of confidence in me, but for whatever reason, somewhere along the way, I forgot how amazing I was and that being me was enough. And although this was tough to write, I figure if it was so easy for me to forget about how great I am then perhaps you needed a reminder of how amazing you are as well. If there is ever a choice between being you and only being liked by a few versus being someone else who is loved by many, always choose to be yourself. The right man will respect your differences and love your flaws. The right woman wouldn't dilute them to begin with.

CHAPTER 7
FOCUS ON FRIENDSHIP

As first dates become second dates and second dates become third ones, your time will soon be consumed by one person. And while this is a fun and exciting time because you are spending time with the one that you think could be the one, it's important during this stage of the relationship to take things slowly. He has passed the interview and even seemed to have made it through the security clearance, but as far as I'm concerned, he is still in the probationary period, so don't be too eager to give him an official title as boyfriend or anything that would cause him to believe that this position in your life has been permanently filled. This chapter is about taking your time in the infancy stage of the relationship, when your emotions are consumed by lust, to ensure that the person you're dating excels at being a friend before promoting him to boyfriend. This isn't the time to be distracted by titles; now is the time to focus on friendship.

At the beginning of a relationship, it's normal to want to define it. In some cases people might even feel pressure to put a label on a status because it makes both parties involved feel more secure with where they stand in each others lives, but doing so prematurely isn't wise. If you give someone an official title before they have proven that they can do the job successfully, you may end up having to terminate them for misconduct or poor performance, which could cost you some valuable resources like tears and time. Calling someone your boyfriend is like going under contract with them emotionally; you immediately start holding them to a standard of your expectation of that role. Statistics show that 80% of people lie about themselves during interviews in order to land a job, and after getting the job, only one in five employees actually pass their probationary periods. I'm sure similar statistics prove true in dating; you never really get the full picture until the "auditions" are over, so why do we feel like we have to define a relationship after a few good dates? People are always going to put on their best face during the first few encounters. Take all of that pressure out of the equation and be transparent about just being friends first. If the person you're seeing is meant to be your husband, he will be; you don't need to rush the process. For now, you just need to be sure of who he is as a person and a friend. Just because he is nice to you and you enjoy hanging out with him doesn't mean he deserves to be your "boyfriend" yet. Remember, you aren't dating for passion; you're dating for purpose - so take your time to ensure that he lines up with what you are seeking in a husband, not a boyfriend.

When I first met my husband, I thought he was very attractive, kind, smart, and he was checking most of the non-negotiables boxes that were on my list. Although he looked really good on paper, I still wanted to take things slowly; so slowly that he asked me to be his girlfriend twice and both times I turned him down. Yes, sis, I really did turn his butt down. I didn't turn him down because I didn't like him; I did like him, but I **loved** me. While I wasn't sure about him yet, I was sure about who I was and what I wanted in life. So I did things my way for a change instead of jumping all in at the first sign of a man's interest in me. I made him wait. And to this day, I don't apologize for it because I wasn't dating for passion. I refused to date him exclusively until I was sure that what we had was in line with my purpose.

The first time he asked me the infamous three words, "What are we?" I was kind of caught off guard because in the past I was typically the one to ask the guys I dated that question. So I simply responded like most guys do: "We're friends." I explained to him that because we live on such a small island and both work in similar industries I didn't want to be associated with him on an intimate level because I had a reputation to protect. I preferred to remain friends until I was sure that this was a relationship I wanted to pursue seriously. He understood and we continued to hang out and get to know each other. The second time we discussed relationships, he expressed to me that he wanted to be my boyfriend officially and exclusively because he was sure of his desires and didn't want to date anyone else but me. Well at this point I still wasn't ready but he wasn't taking no for an answer. He said, "I tell ya what, I'm going to just start calling you my girlfriend whether you like it or not," and I said, "Fine by me, [so] long as you know that I won't be calling you my boyfriend!" We laughed and continued building our friendship and he was happy he was getting closer to unlocking my heart, while I was thrilled that I was finally standing my ground in a relationship. This was so new for me to be in a relationship where someone was actually pursuing me and I didn't have to beg for a place in his life. He was all but begging to fill a position in mine. This was refreshing and I enjoyed getting to know him. I learned that he was a man of his word. I learned that he valued his family and that he had a great relationship with his mother; the way a man treats his mom is very important to me. I learned that he was honest and loyal and everyone who mentioned his name spoke highly of him. During that time, he also demonstrated that nothing was too good for me and he would do whatever it took to make me smile. He didn't need a title for that; he treated me like a queen regardless. It didn't take me much longer to smell the roses and realize that with him was where I wanted to be. I decided to not make him ask me again. One night while he and I were chatting, I casually mentioned that he was my boyfriend and his eyes lit up like I had said he won the lottery. The look said it all; I knew that I had the right candidate for the job but I was grateful I gave myself the time to come to that realization on my own terms, and not because I felt like I had to.

Taking things slowly at a time when your heart is skipping beats is important to the success and future of your relationship. It minimizes the risk of prematurely going under emotional contract with someone who isn't fit to be a friend, let alone a boyfriend. Focusing on friendship allows you to get to know and like a person for who they are, as opposed to what they can do for you. Being good friends in a relationship is far more important than a title you use for people to define you with.

CHAPTER 8
EXPECTATIONS VS. ULTIMATUMS

Everyone in a relationship has an expectation of the other person. One woman's expectation might be that men should always pay on the first date. Another woman's expectation might be that men should open doors for women. Having an idea of what you want, or how you should be treated in a relationship isn't a bad thing, especially if you are used to a certain standard. The problem arises when you don't communicate your expectations early on so that the other person has a fair chance to either meet your standards or let you know where they stand in the event they aren't interested in meeting them. Uncommunicated expectations can disrupt peace in a relationship. Film producer/bestselling author/speaker Devon Franklin once said, "the key to a happy relationship is communicating expectations. One of us has an expectation of the other that we have not communicated, and then we hold them hostage to an uncommunicated expectation, we get upset at them, and then we treat them based upon something that they never had an opportunity to respond to." He couldn't have summed it up any clearer. This happens all the time in relationships and it can easily be avoided if we have the difficult conversations early on.

One of the most common uncommunicated expectations that tend to ruin relationships is how long a woman is willing to wait for a man to commit to her with a proposal. Too often we see relationships that are going so well until one person - usually the woman - feels like she has invested too much of her time into the relationship without the security of a formal commitment. The expectation turns into frustration that eventually leads to an ultimatum, which very rarely ends well. In this situation, the conversation probably sounds similar to this: "Look John, we have been dating for four years now and I love you, but I'm ready to take our relationship to the next phase; I want to be married. I can't see myself continuing on in this relationship without some form of commitment. I'm giving you six months to decide what you're doing or I'm leaving." When relationships get to this point, it's not only unfortunate and demoralizing for a woman to have this conversation but also unfair for the man on the receiving end to be restricted to an ultimatum that he was unprepared for. Expectations, especially the ones that have the potential to turn into ultimatums, should always be communicated early on so that both parties involved have the opportunity to discuss them honestly and openly. Needless to say, in this chapter I will show you how to communicate your expectations regarding the dating timeline so that you can avoid an ultimatum. This is extremely important, as this will play a major role in how soon your man pops the question.

Before I give you the 411 on how I handled the awkward conversation regarding my dating expectations, let me first answer the question that most women want to know: how long is too long to date a man without a promotion to fiancée and wife? The truth is, when it comes to the amount of time you should give a guy to commit before you quit, there is no right or wrong answer - it all depends on what you want out of that relationship. If your intentions are to date for the purpose of marriage, then you probably don't want to date someone who has an aversion to commitment - that would obviously delay the progression of your purpose. But every relationship is different and how long a couple dates before the engagement period can depend on various factors. However, there are expert opinions on how soon is too soon and how long is too long. Marriage therapist and author John Amodeo believes that a marriage proposal that happens within 12 months of dating is too soon (I strongly agree), whereas a proposal that happens anywhere between 12 to 24 months after a couple has already expressed mutual interest and established a desire to pursue a relationship is safe. While I believe that the length of a couple's courtship is entirely up to the couple, and I respect everyone's journey, my advice to you is **don't** do marathon dating! There is no need for you to date someone for 5+ years, especially if you started the relationship in your late 20s. It is common and reasonable for high school/college sweethearts to date for longer periods because of statutory obligations and/or the desire to mature themselves individually before committing. However, there are no excuses for adults who are already established within their careers and know exactly what they want and where they are going. We already know the definition of dating is "a stage of romantic relationships in humans whereby two people meet socially with the aim of each assessing the other's suitability as a prospective partner in an intimate relationship or marriage." It doesn't take years to assess if someone would be a suitable partner. From the moment a man meets a woman, he can tell if she is marriage material and he knows within just a few months of dating her whether or not he would marry her.

It doesn't take years for men to figure that out, so you don't need to feel pressured into giving him "more time"; either he knows or he doesn't, and if he doesn't, he needs to get out of the way so that the one who does can find you. Don't get me wrong, if your bestie and her partner dated for seven years before he popped the question, that's fine; congratulate her for her endurance, but I don't endorse or encourage that for you. Please know that I'm not passing judgment on anyone's relationship progression, I just want to dispel the theory that it takes years for a person to know that they know. With that said, you also can't make a man ready to commit. Either he is ready or he isn't, which is why it's important to not waste time when someone isn't ready. Investing additional years into a relationship with a man who doesn't want to commit won't change the trajectory of his heart. Don't confuse the length of a relationship with the strength of a relationship. It's important to know when it's time to go and at the first sign that a relationship is going nowhere is a good time for you to head elsewhere. You need to know how long you are capable of investing emotionally into a relationship without receiving a return on your investment. The time frame may be different for every woman but know how long is too long for you and be sure to communicate your expectations on this early.

When I was in my mid 20s, I started implementing a two-year rule. The two-year rule basically meant that I could date a man exclusively for two years; however, if a formal commitment wasn't made before the end of that 24-month period, I would have to let him go. During the 24-month period, I would review the relationship every 6 months and the review was an assessment for both myself and my partner where we discussed honestly how we are doing in the relationship, whether both of our needs are being met, things we could improve on, and if we should continue to pursue the relationship further. These questions are extremely important because they are the report card of a relationship. Some relationships drag on for two years when it should have been over within the first five months because instead of addressing things head on, they subconsciously push things aside, hoping and in some cases praying that they would get better. We can't be so desperate to keep love that we are willing to risk our needs in a relationship all for the sake of having a relationship. Set time aside to formally review your relationship. Make it a date; you can do it over wine and artichoke dip, or do it at your home, but it is important to have these conversations.

Communicating your expectations about how long you are capable of dating without a commitment probably isn't a conversation for the first or second date but your expectations should definitely be made known early on. As a matter of fact, when my husband and I decided that we were dating exclusively, I let him know about my two-year rule. I still remember that date, and the conversation, which didn't go as smoothly as I had hoped, but I held my ground anyway. I was firm without being rude and I didn't hold my tongue just because my words were uncomfortable for him to digest. I let him know that I thought he was a great guy, and that I was enjoying where our relationship was headed, but I wanted him to be aware that I didn't do marathon dating and that while I enjoyed his company, I wouldn't be anyone's "girlfriend" for longer than two years. We had already been seeing each other for a few months, so technically he had about a year and nine months left, not that I was counting. Well, he wasn't feeling what I had to say at all; I could feel his mood change and he was almost in defense mode. He explained to me that in his culture it's quite common for a couple to date for anywhere between five to 10 years before considering marriage. I told him that perhaps he should date someone from his country because that wasn't my standard and I wasn't interested in adopting his norm. He also told me that no one would pressure him into marriage. I politely explained that I wasn't pressuring him and I certainly didn't plan to, which is why I wanted to be upfront and honest about my dating expectations. I continued with "If you don't know how you feel about someone after 24 months of dating exclusively and getting to know each other, no amount of time thereafter will help make that more clear. So if a proposal doesn't happen within that time, then I'm obviously not the one for you and I have to let you go so that you can go find your soul mate and get out of the way of the man that wants to marry me." Let's be clear, that isn't pressure; that's transparency. There is a big difference between communicating your expectations versus giving an ultimatum. Being clear about your expectations from the beginning puts everything on the table so that the people at the table can decide whether they want to stay or leave.

Well, after that uncomfortable and very awkward conversation, we still had a great evening and he said he still wanted us to pursue the relationship further, so we continued to date. Ironically about two months later, he told me that he wanted to take me to his country when he goes to visit his family. His family was back in Europe and he only got to visit them once a year, so he expressed to me that if he didn't take me at that moment he wouldn't get the chance to introduce me to them for another year. So I said yes to the trip and four months into our relationship, I was flying across the world to meet his family. I didn't know what the future of our relationship looked like, but at that point I knew he was pretty serious about me. As I said earlier, men know within months whether it's a sure thing or not, and the same man that told me that no one would pressure him into getting married, ended up proposing to me a year later. The first time he took me to his country, I was his girlfriend. The following year he took me as his fiancée and the year after I returned as his wife. When a man knows what he wants, he doesn't need an eternity to decide if you are the one - he decides early on whether you are the one he wants to spend an eternity with.

Did his proposal come as a surprise to me? Absolutely not. The date, time and other logistics of the proposal were a surprise to me of course but the fact that he wanted to marry me wasn't. I knew that he wanted to marry me because when I put my expectations on the table, he stayed at the table. I knew that I was the prize, I knew that I was someone's good thing, and I also knew that if he didn't realize it, someone else would, which is why I had to be stingy with my time. If I hadn't been clear with my husband about my standards and expectations from the beginning, he probably wouldn't have proposed for another four or more years because that was his standard. Being the person that I am, I would have gotten frustrated with him and either thrown in the towel or thrown out an ultimatum. The lesson here is be clear and confident about your standards and expectations early on, and more importantly, be OK if someone isn't interested in meeting your expectations because if they won't someone else will.

CHAPTER 9
SHARING IS NOT CARING

I understand how important sharing content is, especially in the information age where bloggers and social media celebrities are paid more for posts than some attorneys make in a year. But regardless of how much coin your content can bring you, your private life should be left out of your public platforms. If you can't fathom the thought of not sharing romantic details of you and your boo, then at least consider not sharing anything about them until after they have committed to you. The more you share your private life with a public following, the more entitled people will feel to offer their opinions on what you share. Giving hundreds, and in some cases thousands and millions, of followers a stake in your private life can hinder the growth of your relationship. Learn how to keep your relationship private without keeping your partner a secret. This chapter will demonstrate the adverse impact of sharing your private life on social media, and how limiting the information you share on social media can actually strengthen your relationship.

There is nothing more cringe worthy than watching people bounce from relationship to relationship on social media. We've all seen it happen and it's the same pattern every time. One minute homegirl is posting cute pictures with

Jamaal, and they're traveling together and going on romantic dates, and you think you will see engagement photos soon. The next thing you know, she is posting subliminal messages about protecting her heart.

So you go to her page and all of the pictures of her and Jamaal are gone and you're thinking, "Well, that was anticlimactic." Fast forward to nine weeks later and she is posting pictures of her and a new mystery bae in a restaurant, but all you can see is his hand, and your next thought is, "Here we go again." It's only a matter of time before she starts posting his face and #couplegoals pictures before that relationship fizzles out right before our eyes. **Don't** be that girl, sis! Just as uncomfortable as it is for women to see other women on social media jump from relationship to relationship, it is equally as uncomfortable for men to see. Men notice the relationship patterns and trends that play out before them just as much as we do. Just because they don't like, comment, or gossip about it doesn't mean that they don't notice it - and no man wants to feel like they're going to be the next guy to be featured in your social media soap opera. Don't get me wrong, you shouldn't stay in an expired relationship to save face for the 'gram either. If someone isn't right for you, the best thing to do is to let them go; there's no shame in that. Break ups happen; they are a normal part of the dating process. The amount of men you have dated or will date before you meet Mr. Right isn't a big deal; the only people keeping count are your "followers," which is why the entire dating process should be kept private. Keeping your love life private allows you to navigate relationships in peace. Privacy equals peace.

Another drawback of oversharing your private life on social media is that when things don't go according to plan you lose credibility. Most women want to appear as if they have it all together; we all claim to be so smart, with a strong head on our shoulders and a strong spirit of discernment, and our friends will probably even back this up saying the same thing about us. But all of this goes out the window the minute we flaunt our relationships on social media and things go awry. Well honey, if you have such a strong spirit of discernment, how come you couldn't discern that your last boyfriend was a fool before you publicly promoted him? And while we are talking about promoting guys, I would be remiss if I didn't bring this up. Why do some ladies still feel the need to publicly praise their boyfriends for doing ordinary things? Don't post a photo of him and caption it "My #mcm because he's always there for me." Yeah, that's his job; a boyfriend is supposed to be there for his girlfriend; he isn't doing anything extraordinary that you should be praising him publicly. It grinds my gears to see women selling themselves short by doing the most for guys who are literally doing the least. And just so you know, praising him publicly on social media doesn't give him incentive to do real significant things - like actually making you his fiancée - because you are making it clear to him and the world that his ordinary behavior is enough to keep you happy. I mean - have you ever seen a business publicly recognize employees for just doing their job? Nah! But I could just imagine what the newspaper article would read; "XYZ Ltd. would like to acknowledge Mark Hinds for being such an average employee. He has been at the company for five months now and he does everything the job requires of him. If one day he decides to go above and beyond and demonstrates exemplary job performance, we may promote him, but for now we are just thrilled to have him working with us and we want the world to know." Sounds ridiculous right?

Companies only publicly recognize employees that stand out, that go above and beyond what the job requires - people that make the company better than how they met it. You should take the same stance. Always remember that he is vying for the permanent position in your heart so save your public praises for when he really takes your breath away, like when he pops the question perhaps.

You already know when it comes to sharing details about your relationship on social media I strongly advise against it, but if that's a bit too extreme for you then my other rule applies: don't claim him publicly before he claims you. Don't post pictures with him, don't post statuses about him, and don't allude to a relationship of any sort unless he has already done so via his public platforms first. This rule also means that you can't ask him to do so first. Give him the opportunity to show you off without you having to prompt him. See here's the thing, men are hunters, and just because he and you are in a relationship, it doesn't mean that the sport is over. Yes he wants to bring you into his world and show off what he has found but he will do it in his time. When you decide to be eager and share him before he is even ready to be put on display, it can subconsciously make him feel like the hunted rather than the hunter. It also puts unnecessary pressure on your relationship because now he doesn't just have to think of ways to make you happy; he is also now conscious of the 800 other followers that will be judging the flowers he sends you and the restaurants he chooses to take you to. Don't scare him off by sharing too much, too soon. Your relationship is for you, not for public consumption.

Another reason to keep your relationship away from the "limelight" is the mere fact that not everyone that follows you actually likes you. Don't let the likes fool you; you have some followers and "friends" that keep tabs on you just to know your next move. Not everyone will be happy for you when you find happiness and the dangerous thing about social media is that sabotage can be silent. Girls that don't even want your man will slide in his DM's just to disrupt the harmony in your relationship. Why would you give people the ammunition to do that?

In previous relationships, I had always been the one to initiate going public on social media; my reason back then when I was less mature was, "It's not official until it's online." I didn't realize this pattern in my previous relationships until later; I was the one doing the hunting. So when my husband and I were just dating, I made a conscious decision not to make the same mistake again. I kept my pages completely relationship free. Eventually one day he noticed and asked if he could post some photos of him and me on his Facebook page. I let him know that I had no problems with him posting photos of us on his social media but I would wait a little while longer before I took such a step. Ironically my first "relationship" post on Instagram wasn't until after we got engaged. From the outside looking in, it probably seemed as if I went from no relationship to engaged and that's OK because while my life may be an open book my private life isn't. I waited until after I was engaged to share details about my relationship and even then what I share is very limited. I think the fact that I wasn't so eager to claim him publicly made him want to promote me as his lady more. When men aren't chased after, they enjoy the opportunity to chase after what they want.

PART III: HOW TO GET HIM TO COMMIT

CHAPTER 10
NO RISK, NO REWARD

By this stage in your relationship, you should have a pretty good idea of who the person you're dating is. Your foundation would've already been established, your expectations revealed, and your intentions exposed, so it's safe to say that at this stage you care deeply about your partner and probably don't want to lose him. I hate to break it to you but now is the time to give him up. No, no, I'm not telling you to break up with him; what I mean is, you have got to hand the relationship over to God. This chapter is about risking your relationship by submitting it to God for His making or His taking. When you give things to God, He does one of two things, He either makes it greater or He takes it away to give you better. Either way you're winning right? So while your emotions are strong and your dopamine levels are high, go ahead and ask God to have His way with your relationship and to remove your boyfriend from your life if he isn't the husband God has for you. Everything just got real all of a sudden, huh? When I tell women to do this, most women respond with, "But if I pray like that, what if God actually takes him away from me?" And that's the problem right there! If you aren't willing to risk everything for God, He won't have anything to reward you for.

Listen, sis, when you ask God to remove time wasters from your life, He does so, and in my experience He does so expeditiously! And when God speaks, His words are loud and clear; it's just that sometimes we play deaf when he tells us to let go of the things our flesh wants to hold onto. I remember praying that same prayer back when I was dating my ex, and not even a week later, I discovered that my ex was cheating on me. I mean it couldn't have gotten any clearer than that right? Yet still I was negotiating with God like, "Look, I told you to send me a sign and you sent me billboard, I get it, but he has already apologized, and everyone makes mistakes, how about I give him another chance?" Sigh. I'm sure God was up there listening to me like, "You're kidding, right?" And for the record, despite God's clear instructions, I ended up getting back with that cheater. Don't judge me, I made some really dumb decisions back then. Anyway, don't worry; that reconciliation was short lived, and I broke up with him for good shortly thereafter. I brought that up to propose this question: why do we ask God for revelation, and when He shows us, we disregard the message? That's how we end up wounded due to our lack of obedience. If you submit things to God, have enough faith not to pick up the things he has already instructed you to put down.

You might be asking "Why now? Why couldn't I have just done this during the beginning stages of the relationship?" Here's the thing - I encourage everyone to include God in his or her relationships from the beginning, but the reason this is important to do at this latter part of the dating cycle is because not every good relationship is supposed to end in marriage. Just because God allows a relationship to come together doesn't mean that the relationship is designed to stay together. Often people are under the impression that because two people are in a Christian relationship together that the destination of their relationship is marriage. The reality is that sometimes God connects people together for other purposes, some of which can be temporary. As the saying goes, some people come into your life for a reason, some for a season and some for a lifetime. I genuinely thought the relationship I had with my ex was for a lifetime solely because we were both Christians, had similar backgrounds and wanted the same things in life. It was only after I submitted that relationship to God that I received revelation and eventually ended it for good. As it turned out, that union was solely for a season but the purpose of that relationship was for the maturation of my faith. When you get to the stage where you think you have found the one, give him to God.

Now fast-forward to my current relationship. When I noticed things were getting serious and I was truly starting to fall for the guy who I now call husband, I knew what I had to do. I knew I had to hand my relationship over to God for His making or His taking. So I decided to fast and pray this prayer:

"I submit my relationship to you God. I know you have connected me with this man for a reason. I believe that you placed me in his life to bring him closer to you, and if that is my only purpose in his life then let me know when my job is done, but God if my purpose in his life is to be his wife, then make that known to him and give him the boldness to make me his wife. Father God, I love him but I love You more. I want to walk in Your will, so if he isn't the husband that you have hand-picked for me, then please remove him from my life quickly."

I prayed this throughout the course of my relationship. And while I waited for signs and revelations that could alter the course of my relationship, all God sent me was peace. And I often wondered why God was being so silent when I was being so fervent. It only dawned on me recently that God wasn't speaking to me because He was speaking to my husband showing him that I was his good thing. After you submit the relationship to God, you will know that you have found Mr. Right if you aren't the one receiving instruction concerning that relationship. See, in my previous relationship, when I submitted it to God, God spoke to me directly, and His instructions were clear, so I ended it; but when I submitted my current relationship to God, God spoke directly to my husband who acted according to God's instructions. The person receiving instructions from God in a relationship changes based on the purpose of that relationship. Hence why submitting your relationship to God, even after you think you have found the one, is important to the revelation of God's purpose for that relationship.

Giving your relationship to Christ for His will to be done is risky business because the outcome might not always be what you want at the time, but it will always be in your favor. God never removes anything without a plan to reinstate something greater. In some cases, you may have to wait a while before your greater comes; in other cases it may be quick. No matter what, His plan is always better than anything we can create for ourselves.

CHAPTER 11
WHAT GOES IN, COMES OUT

Anything that you feed has the opportunity to grow but what you feed it determines whether it flourishes, or if it withers and dies. If you feed a plant with the right nutrients, it can grow into an entire field; conversely if you feed a plant with salt water, it can become dehydrated and eventually wither and die. If you feed a child the right foods, the child can grow into an adult; but if you feed a child with only baby food forever, the child will become malnourished and his lifecycle would be stunted. The same applies to relationships; what you feed into it affects what you get out of it. I'm not talking about physical food. This chapter is about the spiritual foods that you feed your relationship and the effect it has on its development. Filling your relationship with the right nutrients will bring you one step closer to your man popping the question you have been waiting to hear.

I don't believe that you can force a relationship to lead to marriage but I do believe that the right relationship can be molded into marriage with adequate spiritual consumption. The people you do life with, the shows you watch, the music you listen to and the people you follow on social media are all things that your mind consumes. Needless to say, what transpires in your life is a direct result of what happens in your mind. You have to be intentional about what you and your partner consume mentally together and apart. When I started to think back on my previous failed relationship, and I really analyzed the cause of death of that relationship, I realized that the union was severely spiritually malnourished. It had been starved to death. We were both Christians but we surrounded ourselves with non-believers. We attended separate churches. Most of our friends were single and uninterested in serious relationships. The relationship advice he got came from his "boys" - a group of guys from broken homes raised with broken hearts and trust issues. Most of the relationship advice I got came from my girlfriends, most of whom were either single or in and out of relationships. Needless to say, it's pretty obvious to me now that what that relationship was being fed was more like fast food or take-out, not gourmet.

So, how can you feed your relationship spiritually? Well, you first have to be spiritually full on your own. If you aren't spiritually full, you won't be able to feed anyone or anything else. When you are in a place where you are constantly being filled with the spirit of God, the relationship you are in will feed off of your overflow. But don't be fooled, your overflow is only a snack; it won't be enough to sustain the growth of a relationship, so you will need to be intentional about feeding your relationship in different ways. Below are the four nutrients I fed my relationship with that kept it full, healthy and flourishing from dating to married.

1. Go to Church Together - if you are in a serious committed relationship and you are going to separate churches, it's time to have a conversation about whose church will be your church home together. You need to join his church, he needs to join yours, or you both need to find a new church where you can be comfortable worshipping together. When you attend separate churches, you may receive separate teachings; and when you try to apply two doctrines to one relationship, there can be a disconnect in companionship. Worshipping together connects a couple on a deeper level and brings harmony to your walk with Christ together. Studies have also proven that couples tend to be happier when there is joint church attendance as opposed to going to separate churches or when one

partner isn't attending any church at all. When my husband and I were dating, the church that I was attending at the time wasn't really his cup of tea, so we went church shopping and eventually found a great church that made both of us feel at home. After we started worshipping together, we were able to unpack the lessons we learned on Sunday mornings and apply them to our daily lives. We are often on one accord because we heard the same thing at the same time in the same context. We look forward to our post-church brunch conversations where we digest God's word even more and discuss how we can apply it in our own lives.

2. Get Involved in Church Together – there are various ways to get plugged in at church, but I highly recommend joining a small group, also known as a Bible study group. Most churches offer several small group options. Some are dedicated to women only; some are for teens, couples, and so on. I recommend joining a small group that you and your partner can go to together. A small group is where you can pour out your heart regarding real issues and be poured

back into with spiritual wisdom and guidance. They will hold you and your partner accountable and make sure your relationship is a reflection of God. If an issue arises within your relationship, don't go to your girlfriends to talk about it; go to your small group to pray about it. The small group that my husband and I are a part of has played a huge role in our spiritual consumption. Our small group is our source of safety, conviction and motivation to have a relationship that pleases God.

3. Read Books Together – reading together on the subject of love, relationships, spirituality and even marriage can elevate your perception on those topics. In fact, books are a great way to introduce ideas into your daily conversations, which will take root into your relationship in a deeper way. Create your own little book club between you and your partner by assigning yourselves reading and having serious topical dialogue about how each pertinent lesson can be applied in your relationship. If you or your partner isn't too keen on reading, then a 300-page book might not be the right option for you. Start by sending

each other articles and have meaningful discussions about them. I wasn't an avid reader but I did appreciate knowledge. My husband, on the other hand, loves reading and is always sending me articles to digest. I try to read everything he sends me, especially if it's on the topic of relationships, and we make time to go over the intriguingly thought-provoking pieces we discover together.

4. Find Friends That Are Happily Married – whether it happens through your church, work or social circles, be intentional about connecting with other couples that are in happy marriages. When you start hanging out as a couple with other couples that enjoy their marriage, it subconsciously brings marriage to the forefront of your man's thoughts. It won't happen immediately but it does happen eventually. The more mutual friends you have that are in fruitful wedded relationships, the higher the chances are that your man will want to commit. Why? Because you will be the couple that everyone wants to see married next, so your friends will be the ones making comments that add a little positive pressure

to your relationship, which is great because you will never have to. The idea is to get people to do the hard work for you without you even having to ask them. Men don't like being pressured by women on the subject of engagement or marriage but when his married guy friends make him feel like he's missing out on something, he will want to get to that next level quicker than he would have on his own willpower. When we were still dating, my husband and I often hung out with this group of friends who were all married couples; we love them and still enjoy their company to this day, but at the time, when we were dating, they always brought up the fact that we weren't in the "club" yet. One night the guys were chatting and one of them looked at my husband and said, "Sorry mate, you can't be a part of this conversation; this is married men talk." My husband laughed and said, "No worries, I'll be there soon."

The jokes and the banter we endured as the "unmarried couple" were harmless but oh so appreciated on my end because it made my life easy. Remember, the key here is to find couples that are in happy marriages because if they aren't the adverse effect can occur as what goes in is what you will get out. Your relationship, just like anything else you want to see grow, needs the proper nourishment. What you feed into it will determine whether it flourishes into the next stage of its lifecycle, or whether it weakens until there is no more life. A plant may sprout with just water but it will take a whole lot more to make it bloom. Focus on the fertilizer that feeds your relationship.

CHAPTER 12
DON'T PLAY WIFEY

Well, here we are, the final chapter. These are the last points I'm going to share with you because there really isn't much more to this dating thing anyway. You already had the magic and now you have the way. The reason I saved this point for last is because I believe that understanding this principle and not compromising on it is what caused my husband to pop the question as soon as he did. The title is telling, but if you haven't figured it out, this chapter is about overcoming the urge to give a boyfriend the benefits of a husband.

I mean we all know the saying "Why buy the cow when you can get the milk for free," right? Mom used to preach that to us all the time when she dished out her unsolicited dating advice to my sister and me. As annoying as it is to hear that saying, it is still very true and very relevant to the way men think today. What incentive does a man have to marry a woman if he is already gaining the benefits of a wife without any sacrifice? Don't, and I repeat don't, play the role of a wife to a boyfriend; doing so only delays the destination of your relationship. Either he wants to marry you, or he doesn't, but playing house with him won't help him decide. Look, if he hasn't put a ring on it yet, then he is still auditioning for a permanent position in your life, so don't treat him like he has already earned the spot. I mean, seriously sis, would an employer give a bonus check to a temporary employee? Heck nah! Bonuses are reserved for permanent personnel. If you want to see your relationship progress into marriage sooner rather than later, don't give a man his bonuses before earned.

Some of the "wife benefits" I recommend to stay away from until after the proposal are cooking, cleaning, doing his laundry, sex, and moving in. Cooking is one of the subtle bad habits that women tend to spoil their boyfriends with most. For some women it's one of those things you dive into because you genuinely enjoy it; for others you just want to show him that you can throw down in the kitchen to prove that you actually are wife material. Whatever the case may be, doing this so often that it becomes your duty and an expectation from your man is only delaying your proposal. Now don't get me wrong, I'm not opposed to cooking for your boo, but it should be a treat and he should also reciprocate the favor in cooking for you on occasion, even if it's a turkey and cheese sandwich. I personally love cooking. I also love that my husband loves my cooking. It not only makes me feel good about myself but also makes me want to cook for him all the time! The way he licked his fingers after I killed it with the curry chicken and white rice made me feel like a Top Chef All Star. But even then, I had to be intentional not to let those feelings trick me into becoming his personal chef. So in between going out for dinner, I cooked for him and some nights he cooked for me. One night he cooked for me, he accidentally set the oven on fire - long story - but at no point during our courtship was I the main source of his meals. Slaving in a kitchen for a man that isn't physically or fiscally responsible for you is irresponsible. You can show off your skills and cook him a meal or two every now and then but don't let him get used to it. Don't spoil him with a daily food service until he is ready to officially make you a part of his daily life.

As it relates to doing your boyfriend's house chores, the rules are simple, don't! Leave that up to his mama. We all get the same 24 hours in the day. If you're responsible for keeping your house tidy, then he should do the same for his. I don't know any women who particularly enjoy cleaning. I mean let's be honest, when someone asks what you enjoy doing in your spare time, is cleaning ever in the top five answers? Heck nah!

So why give a guy the impression that you do by doing his dirty work without compensation? No woman has ever been proposed to because of how well they can work a mop. Well. . .never mind! But I know women who don't even live with their boyfriends and they will still make time to go to their guy's house to sweep, mop, wash and fold their laundry. This will always baffle me. My rule has always been: a man has to put a ring on my finger before I lift a finger to clean his house. I don't love cleaning but I'm a bit of a neat freak, so it's second nature to keep my living space tidy; expect the same from anyone you date. Eventually when my relationship got to the stage where my husband invited me over to his place to cook for me, I remember walking into his apartment thinking, "This is nice, well-appointed, looks and smells relatively clean," so I got comfortable and took my shoes off. As I walked over to the couch I could feel dust and grit collect underneath my bare feet with every step I took. Yuck! In my head I said, "Jeez, clean up much?" Anyway, I decided to be a good houseguest and enjoy the evening despite the dirt but this cleaning issue needed to be addressed! I didn't want to hurt his feelings but eventually I had to let him know. I told him that I loved hanging out with him and I enjoyed spending time at his place, but if he wanted me to continue coming there, he would have to hire a cleaning lady. He worked six days a week, so I knew that deep cleaning his house weekly wasn't a realistic expectation of him and I certainly wasn't volunteering to clean his place for him because it was outside of the requirements of my role as girlfriend. So he hired a weekly cleaning service. His house was clean; he was happy; I was happy. Most importantly, my time wasn't being exploited for the purpose of him seeing me as "wifey material."

When it comes to sex, I would advise you to wait until marriage. I'm definitely not the poster girl for purity, so I won't get all self-righteous here, but there is a reason God designed marriage to prelude sex. As the Bible says, sex causes two people to become one. Your body, once given away can't be taken back. While you can train your mind to forget a memory, it's hard to train your body not to crave a feeling, which is why it's dangerous to let passion get ahead of purpose. Don't run the risk of physically connecting with someone that isn't a part of your lifetime journey. A lot of women are still under the impression that if they don't give it up a man is less likely to pursue a relationship with them and that's false - I am proof of it. Some men will be turned off by your standards but standards only scare boys with bad intentions. A man that intends on marrying you won't mind waiting. After my husband and I got engaged, we knew we didn't want to wait until our wedding day which was still 11 months away, so what did we do? We got married 5 months earlier than our wedding. We had a private ceremony in the middle of our living room - me, him, the pastor and our parents. We still enjoyed our big, beautiful wedding several months later in front of friends and family but we felt good that we had done the right thing. The man God has for you won't need a test drive unless it's the car he's buying you. Make him wait. Men like instant gratification but what they truly crave is endurance.

On the subject of moving in, unless you get the ring, don't do any such thing! Moving in together before there is a formal commitment gives couples a comfort level that only distracts and delays them from their purpose. And what is the purpose of moving in with your partner if the intention isn't to spend the rest of your life with them? And if that's the intention, then why not just get married? But hey, I'm from the Caribbean, so my take on the subject may be a little different. Speaking of which, it's normal in my culture for unmarried adults to live at home with their parents regardless of their age. Typically, you only move out after you get married or if you decide to purchase your own home. Needless to say, I lived with my parents during my courtship with my husband, and although I had my own car, when we went on dates, my husband would pick me up from my parents' house and then drop me off at the end of the evening. He thought it was bizarre that I still lived with my parents and he asked me to move in with him several times, which I refused. Despite my refusal to move in with him, he gave me a key to his apartment. When he gave me the key, I knew he was serious about our future together but I also knew that this was no time to cave in, so I held my ground. I continued to live with my parents. I kept the key though and I popped in on him every now and again just to make sure everything was kosher; don't judge me. One date night as he was dropping me back off to my parents, he lamented to me that he hated not living with me and that picking me up from my parents' house was the best part of his day but dropping me off afterward was the worst part of his day. The feelings were mutual but I couldn't cave in and good thing I didn't. About a month later he proposed.

After I got engaged, one of my girlfriends approached me at an event and asked, "How on Earth did you pull this off? I have been dating my boyfriend for five years. I cook, clean and I pull out all the stops in the bedroom and he still won't commit. You basically just started dating this guy and you are already engaged?" At that point I just smiled and shrugged but what I wanted to tell her was that she was doing a phenomenal job at being a wife - the problem was she was just his girlfriend. She was being taken for granted because she was giving her man the benefits of a husband when he had only applied for the position of a boyfriend and clearly he didn't want a promotion or he would have proposed. But he hung onto the gig anyway, as some men do when they don't know what they want. Here's the thing, it may be up to the men to promote their position in our lives, but it's up to us to demote them when we realize that they aren't up for the job. I hope she reads my book.

Women are givers naturally and men are typically takers - it's just how they are wired. If I had volunteered to cook all the time and clean for my husband while we were just dating, he would have let me. If I had moved in with him and allowed him to enjoy all of me, all the time, he would have accepted it. A man is hardly going to say "don't move in with me yet, you deserve better than this; let's wait until I'm sure you're the one." No, many men are takers and if you give them an inch, they will take a yard. The point is not to give them more than you can afford to lose. As for me, I can't afford to lose time not appreciated. You don't get what you deserve in relationships; you get what you demand. And in this case demanding isn't commanding - it's simply standing for what you believe in without compromise. So my challenge to you as you go forth to flourish in your current or next relationship is this: demand more, command less, stand for something and fall for nothing.

CONCLUSION: HAPPILY EVER AFTER

By now I'm sure you've realized, this book isn't about landing the ring or even finding Mr. Right. It's a lesson on self-worth. It's about you, it's about me and it's about what we teach the women that will come after us. We have been tricked into believing that the phrase "happily ever after" signifies a happy ending that only happens after a prince has found his princess. And in most cases the prince saves his princess from a life that's inadequate because he isn't in it. But that's the problem with fairytales; they couldn't be further from reality. For starters we are Queens, not Princesses. Secondly, we don't need saving; we're not in despair. Third, when your King finds you, he will find you already living your happily ever after. He won't be the completion to a happy ending; he will be an addition to a happy story in progress.

Another reason I don't like fairytales is they never show you the story that comes after happily ever after. So we never know if those love stories even stood the test of time. They just build us up to this crazy idea that once you make it down the aisle with your dream guy, you've had your happy ending. But marriage isn't the finish line. The reality is, it's just the beginning of a race. And the race isn't a sprint. It's a long-distance triathlon that will require you and your partner to ride over rugged terrain, swim through troubled waters and run the race even when you're weary. And what they don't tell you is if the partner you start the race with isn't strong enough to complete it with you, you may end up running it alone. So I'm here to tell you to take your time. There is no hurry. It's better for you to walk alone than to settle for someone that might not be able to complete the journey. It's not about how you start; the beauty in the journey is how you end.

So what will your happily ever after look like? More importantly, if your happily ever after doesn't include a King, will you still live happily? I certainly hope so but that's up to you to decide. Happiness is not a birthright. It's something that you deserve but it isn't owed to you by anyone. It's not something that can be found - it has to be created. In fact, it is your duty to create. So create it. If you don't know where to begin, then start by finding love. How do you find love? Just look in the mirror. You were created in the very image of love - fearfully and wonderfully. While marriage is a beautiful thing, it's in your singleness that you will experience love at its simplest. Self love. God's love. Your happily ever after is already in progress - it's happening right now all around you, so stop waiting for it and start living it.

ABOUT JENA

Born in The Bahamas, raised in The Turks & Caicos and educated in the US, Europe & Asia - Jena Janse is a woman of the world. Although a colorful upbringing has gained her international experience, she considers the Turks & Caicos her only home. The former Sales & Marketing manager turned entrepreneur enjoys serving a diverse community as a life strategist, marketing consultant, writer and speaker, but her favorite role thus far is being a wife.

FUN FACTS: Jena is innately happy. She loves traveling, reading, sailing and tasting wine. Jena has a genuine passion for people and lives by the mantra: if I had one wish, I would give people the ability to see themselves through God's eyes - only then would they realize how magnificent they really are.

References

Complete. (n.d.) Merriam-Webster. Retrieved from
https://www.merriam-webster.com/dictionary/complete

Dating. (2018, September 7). Wikipedia. Retrieved from
https://en.wikipedia.org/wiki/Dating

Derosa, D. B. (2014, April 5). Urban Dictionary. Retrieved from
https://www.urbandictionary.com/Situationship

Neal, A. (2014, August 6). Aiden Neal. Retrieved from
http://aidanneal.com/2014/08/06/9-signs-youre-situationship/

Whole. (n.d.) Oxford Living Dictionaries. Retrieved from
https://en.oxforddictionaries.com/definition/whole